APOCALYPSE
THE BOOK OF REVELATION

APOCALYPSE
THE BOOK OF REVELATION

With a Preface by Prof. Randall Balmer
With an Introduction by Rev. Philemon D. Sevastiades
Translated and with Notes by
Rev. Mark B. Arey with Rev. Philemon D. Sevastiades
Edited by Patra McSharry Sevastiades

THE MILLENNIUM TRANSLATION PROJECT SERIES

The Oracle Publishing Group's
Dayspring Press
Oradell, NJ

Published in 2003 by The Oracle Publishing Group, Inc.
690 Kinderkamack Road, Oradell, NJ 07649

The cover image is a photograph of a facsimile of the Apocalypse from the Codex Sinaiticus: Petropolitanus. Reprinted by permission of Oxford University Press.

Library of Congress Cataloging-in-Publication Data

Bible. N.T. Revelation. English. Arey. 2002.
  Apocalypse : the book of Revelation / with a preface by Randall Balmer ; with an introduction by Philemon D. Sevastiades ; translated and with notes by Mark B. Arey with Philemon D. Sevastiades.
     p. cm. -- (Millennium translation project series)
  ISBN 1-932122-00-1 (hard) -- ISBN 1-932122-01-X (pbk.) -- ISBN 1-932122-02-8 (special ed.)
  I. Arey, Mark B. II. Sevastiades, Philemon D. III. Balmer, Randall Herbert. IV. Title. V. Series.
  BS2823 .A7 2002
  228'.05209--dc21
                                                    2002013987

Manufactured in the United States of America

CONTENTS

PREFACE

This fresh translation of the *Book of Revelation* allows us to see a wonderfully complex book with new eyes. Numerous theological implications, both in doctrine and practice, derive from the manner in which various faith groups understand the New Testament. The American Protestant understanding of Christian belief, especially among those who call themselves "Bible-believing" Christians, may in fact include doctrines influenced by the specific translations used, which in turn are determined by the religious and theological predilections of the translators. Owing to the availability of many versions of the New Testament in the original Greek, different English-language Bibles can and often do support varying religious assertions.

What follows in these pages is an "Orthodox" translation of the *Book of Revelation*. That is to say, the translators have proceeded with an Orthodox hermeneutic process and have applied this to the living text of the Greek Orthodox Church. Because the Eastern Christian traditions are generally overlooked in the West, the Eastern Christian understandings derived from these texts are largely unknown among Western Christians.

The Constantinopolitan text of the New Testament is the product of an ancient, large and diverse textual tradition. The 1904 edition of that text, on which this new translation is based, is an official edition of the New Testament in the Great Church of Christ—that is, an edition published by the Ecumenical Patriarchate of Constantinople and used by all the Churches within its jurisdiction. The New Testament of the Greek-speaking Orthodox Church is a "living" text, used by a large body of believers, those who are part of the Greek Orthodox Church throughout the world. There has never been an "official" translation of this text into English; thus, no single English translation has been approved by the Synod of Constantinople for use by its Churches throughout the English-speaking world.

American Protestants are fond of saying that they hearken back to early Christian practice, because they follow the New Testament as their only source of authority. This translation derives from the most ancient, continuous faith tradition in Christendom, one that adheres to the body of Patristic Tradition by which Orthodox Christianity understands the meaning of the text. Thus the translators believe that they have conveyed the original intentions of the inspired writer, one of the earliest Christians, who spoke and wrote Greek.

The translators have attained here a readability that invites comparison with the literary levels of the finest literature. At the same time, they have employed contemporary idioms so that the text bears a fresh and, at times, stunning "newness." The translators have avoided the familiar phrases of previous English translations while retaining the clarity with which some of these have already illuminated the New Testament in English.

The *Book of Revelation* is exciting again.

Randall Balmer
Ann Whitney Olin Professor of American Religion
Barnard College, Columbia University

INTRODUCTION

"The fatal is always an anticipation of the end in the beginning, a precession of the end whose effect is to topple the system of cause and effect. It is a temptation to pass to the other side of the end, to go beyond this horizon, to deny this perpetually future state of things."

—Jean Baudrillard, *The Ecstasy of Communication*

The *Apocalypse* was the last book to be accepted as part of the canon of the New Testament. It is the first book of the New Testament to be released by the Millennium Translation Project. The Project is an unprecedented attempt to translate into contemporary literary English the living textual tradition of Orthodox Christianity. The Constantinopolitan Text of 1904, the text on which the Millennium Translation Project is based, is a synodally approved narrative version of the Orthodox Christian Gospel Lectionary tradition. It is still read and preached in Greek Orthodox Churches throughout the world. It is a living text, in the original New Testament Greek, that is directly linked, in every "jot and tittle," to the manuscripts that were so carefully copied and transported from one Christian faith community to another in late antiquity.

For Orthodox Christians, Orthodox Christianity is the living church of Jesus Christ, the inheritor of an unbroken transmission of Christian faith from the Apostles through and in time. The Greeks who are Orthodox Christians are the living descendants, physically and spiritually, of those Christians to whom Paul first preached and wrote in Corinth, Thessalonica, Ephesus, Athens, and so on. That is why Greek Orthodoxy lays unique claim to Christianity, for it has maintained an unbroken tradition of faith for nearly two millennia.

The New Testament canon closed around the beginning of the fifth century in the Common Era (CE); since those centuries of discussion, the *Apocalypse* has become the book most likely to engender opinionated discussion or lunatic-fringe hysteria about Christian beliefs. Luther did not like the *Apocalypse* and would have excluded it from the canon. Zwingli and Calvin expressed similar displeasure with it. Eventually, they addressed its inclusion. It remains an irony of history, then, that among Evangelical Christians, who are in many ways the spiritual descendants of those who led the charge in the Reformation, the *Apocalypse* is frequently understood and revered as a terrifying road map of the future. One can find preachers who cite the text as a divine blueprint of time's terminus and direly conclude that the end of

existence is imminent. This common interpretation of the *Apocalypse* usually features the vengeful return of a Jesus Christ whose patience with humanity has run out. Some few of these same preachers have claimed to possess a special, often "hidden," knowledge of the End Times. However, the *Apocalypse* is a complex document that merits a more thoughtful assessment.

Revealing Fears and Hopes

To begin to understand the *Apocalypse*, one needs first to uncover its historical and cultural context. The cultural milieu in which Christianity forged its self-understanding was the Roman Empire. First and foremost a pagan world, the Roman Empire was simultaneously the epicenter of Hellenistic culture and a melting pot of diverse, even competing traditions of Judaism. A complex dynamic existed within that world of philosophical ferment, and that in turn informed how the texts that gradually came to comprise the definitive New Testament were understood by believers. Therefore, the tendency of each generation to read the *Apocalypse* as a message specific to itself must be tempered by the knowledge that the *Apocalypse* was written and proclaimed for the benefit of the generation that first received it. In addition, apocalyptic literature already

was widespread in the period of the emergence of Christianity and in the period between the two Testaments (c. 250 BCE–55 CE). The apocalyptic genre was represented in the textual traditions of many religions of the time, both pagan and Jewish. That the Apostle John, or Christ Himself, would convey a message using its familiar tropes is therefore most understandable.

Further, by the time the *Apocalypse* was written, probably around 100 CE, some of the faithful were experiencing growing fears because Jesus Christ had not yet returned as promised. Concern over the fate of those dying before Christ's return was one focus of Paul's first letter to the believers in Thessalonica. Of all the documents contained in the New Testament, this letter is believed to have been written first. Fifty years later, John revealed a new fate for those left alive at the return of Christ. Indeed, he may have revealed the second coming of Christ—the Parousia—itself as a spiritual reality for all the faithful.

In exile on Patmos for preaching the Gospel, the Apostle John conveys a message of hope for the afflicted. Believers are reassured that on the throne sits Christ Jesus, who promised He would return, and that those afflicting them will be defeated. The *Apocalypse* becomes a message of hope for those waiting for fulfillment and

vengeance upon those causing persecution, and a guarantee of future triumph in the revelation of what is expected of the persecuted faithful and what they should be doing to attain the Kingdom of God.

Along with the admonitions of the letters to the individual churches in the *Apocalypse*, the supernatural quality of the here and now was being revealed to a faithful populace who were facing rather unpleasant material realities, living in abject fear of the news and rumors of hideous persecutions of their fellow followers elsewhere. Therefore, the text must be read in that light, the light of mingled joy and fear in the witness of martyrs and others whose deaths have precipitated concerns about Jesus' delayed return, even as their noble deaths attest to the genuineness of faith in Christ's promises to them.

Interpretation and Translation

A new translation always begs the question: Why another? Clearly, a translation of the *Apocalypse* based solely upon the living text of the Eastern Orthodox Church is one important answer. Another is the larger question of the interpretation and meaning of Scripture. In the West, this has become idiosyncratic, largely derived from the King James Version, the Revised Standard Version, and

the New Revised Standard Edition, and caught up in the debates regarding the "purity" of textual traditions and the inclusion of alternative readings. The Orthodox Church, which has maintained a coherent textual tradition through its worship and traditions, believes that it understands more than simply the meanings of the words of the text; it believes that it understands the use of the text—how the text should be applied to the faith of its readers.

This is the heart of the issue, after all: Does the new translation change how we understand the original text, and does it better or more closely convey the intention of the author? When it comes to the *Apocalypse*, this is an awesome question. If one is a true believer, then the reason why this is so is self-evident. The Greek Orthodox Church, which has preserved the original texts of the New Testament in the manner closest to their origins, can claim perhaps a larger portion of the fruit of its truths. It has maintained for posterity the text's message and provided a way to understand the text's perceived truths through time by means of its liturgical and historical Tradition: the complex of interpretive tools, faith lived-out and expressed in worship, and the many other characteristics that Tradition comprises. To approach the text with a different agenda is to turn it into something

other than it was intended to be for the followers for whom it was written. Pretenders are free to interpret the *Apocalypse* as they wish, but there is such a thing as a true inheritor, one who has a valid claim of descent. Greek-speaking Orthodox Christians take some justifiable pride in the gift of having the New Testament available in the language of its authors and their ancestors, who were among the first to read and hear the words that revealed a new Truth to the entire world.

Bringing the liturgically living text of the Greek-speaking Orthodox Christian world to Western awareness for the first time in a contemporary and wholly "new" translation will hopefully open the minds of many for whom the two or three most popular English translations have shaped their understanding of the text. The effect of language upon the interpretation of text and the subsequent understanding of theology for Christians cannot be overestimated. More than a few Western Christians have realized that unless one reads the New Testament in the original Greek, one is reading a theological interpretation. Every translation is influenced by the translator's choices, and each translator is influenced by his or her understanding of doctrine and history.

The early Christian community, self-defining its raison d'etre as eschatological in both nature and

purpose, embedded into the Christian ethos a persistent expectation of something extraordinary, a sea-change to the natural expectations of life. They understood that Christ's promise was one of glory that would transform them, make them better, and free them from suffering; that glory was already present, already at work, and they were moving within it and it within them. However, one would be remiss to insist that this was the only purpose and expression of Christian transformation.

Among Eastern Orthodox Christians, the theology of "theosis" or divinization is, arguably, the apex of theological development, the Mt. Tabor of spiritual purpose. The Christian East understood this divine transformation as taking effect in this life, not just the next. The early Christians of the East, therefore, did not focus on eschatological fears but on the hope that each day would bring a greater flowering of the Holy Spirit's presence. In this light and with this understanding they came to include, reluctantly at first, the text of the *Apocalypse* in the New Testament of Jesus Christ. With this in mind and heart we present a new translation into English, reflecting so far as possible the Orthodox Christian truths that the Church's unbroken ecclesiastical traditions have so carefully preserved.

Orthodox Christians believe that they live for Christ

now; they are not waiting for signs of a Christ still to come. In fact, for Eastern Orthodox Christians, the true Revelation is the continuing revelation of Jesus Christ in the world. His presence is ongoing. Orthodox Christians are taught to live for today, in today, seeking the continuing revelation of Christ in the present. Irrespective of when Christ comes for a second time, by living in Christ in the present, one will be ready.

As a result, Eastern Christians do not have a history of calculating the year and date of Christ's return as some Western Christians do. And the ominous connotation of, for example, the number "666" is a Western phenomenon. The Orthodox Christian does not fear a future that includes the Number of the Beast but instead is perpetually wary, as those who live in the material world should be, of all those who today are doers of the Evil One's terrible word.

Interpretation of the *Apocalypse* is also influenced by Orthodox Christian liturgical practice. The "living Church" dwells within the earthly reflection of that perfect and ceaseless worship that transpires in Heaven. This is precisely the importance of the *Apocalypse* for Eastern Christians—it is a model of the nature of our participation in the Kingdom of God here and now and for all of eternity's tomorrows.

One of the delightful discoveries in the *Apocalypse* is that, in the original Greek, John's use of the language conveys a startling aspect: the Greek text is insistent upon the immanent now. To understand the *Apocalypse* is to realize its truth in an ever-present now. It proclaims again and again that salvation and transformation are occurring today; for in Orthodoxy, salvation is not an event, but a process. The change in human being because of Christ's resurrection and return is happening already in a perpetual present. He is the same yesterday, today, and forever.

The cumulative effect of John's choice of language is telling: The perpetual immanence of the *Apocalypse* is not, finally, a glimpse of the future. The *Apocalypse* reveals the ever-present in-breaking of the Kingdom of God, the ceaseless worship and praise that occur in heaven perpetually and on earth when the faithful pray together. There is an eternal and ever-present interaction between heaven and earth. This state of being, described in the *Apocalypse*, is the fulfillment of Jesus' sacrifice and Christ's resurrection. The *Apocalypse* describes and the Divine Liturgy unveils that Jesus Christ has transformed and is transforming human being and, indeed, all of creation. The *Apocalypse* is not a map of the past or future but a revelation of the eternally present.

The Divine Liturgy and the Apocalypse Revealed

Western Christians often state that they believe in the literal meaning of Scripture. Many Orthodox theologians would counter that Orthodox Christianity actually exceeds Western Christianity in its literal understanding of Scripture. It is not surprising, for instance, that the Orthodox interpretation of the *Apocalypse* has been influenced by the liturgical practice of the Orthodox Church, for that liturgical practice was deeply influenced by the *Apocalypse*. Orthodox Christians have realized the *Apocalypse* in the most literal terms possible: The *Apocalypse* is the door through which we pass into the Divine Liturgy. We enter the heavenly Jerusalem each time we celebrate the Divine Liturgy. The Rapture is our departure from this world and our participation in the heavenly revealed Kingdom of God. The altar, embedded with the relics of a saint, is the nexus between this world and the next. The presbyters (priests) are gathered there, around the tomb of the saints, burning incense and praising God (Rev. 5:8).

The *Apocalypse* is the living icon of Orthodox Christianity's belief in a transformative truth, one that affects everyone who follows Christ. Through the Divine Liturgy, we are the recipients of the Church's apostolically authorized distribution of God's grace and of Christ

Himself. For the Orthodox Christian, then, there is a "Parousia" of Jesus Christ on a supernatural level during the Divine Liturgy. When celebrating the Divine Liturgy, each Orthodox Christian is at the "end of time," participating in the eternal and timeless Kingdom of Heaven.

Distinct similarities exist between what many perceive as the post-Christian society of the contemporary West and the post-pagan society of the early Church. Christianity's current self-image as besieged by modernity resonates to the post-pagan Christian sense of persecution and imminent death. The diverse currents in Western Christianity have ignited complex struggles concerning the Christian self-image and called into question the entire enterprise of Christian belief. Many Americans believe that America is at the forefront of a worldwide Christian society, bearing the stamp of the believers who wrote the civil scriptures upon which American governance is based. Others have adopted a "post-Christian" Christianity, whose ethics have superseded the dogmatic beliefs from which they were originally derived.

Christians of diverse beliefs share reactive responses to the images within the *Apocalypse*. The content of those responses are different, but the dynamic of interpretation is, in fact, quite similar. Text is quoted and then

interpreted. Meaning is ascribed and contextualized for the believer. There is a constant search for meaning, or an attempt to neutralize the relevance of competing meanings. In every case, affirmation of truth or the demonstration of irrelevance requires one to assess how successfully the text has been understood. In the diverse multiculturalism of a global society, believers of all stripes are looking for the context in which to understand the meaning of the *Apocalypse*. The earliest Christians, too, searched for a context for their faith within their sacred text, Scripture (bearing in mind the centuries it took to form a common canon). Then as now, the interpretation of the *Apocalypse* as either a revelation of the future or a revelation of current truth will directly affect the manner in which Christian faith is lived out by those who call themselves Christian.

The very first Christians were perhaps the very first post-modernists. They came to believe that the transcendent enactment of Christ's commandment, the literal belief in the words "those who eat My Flesh and drink My Blood abide in Me and I in them" (John 6:56), was to recreate the Truth depicted within the text of the *Apocalypse*. At their most apocalyptic, they no longer had any use for the reference of history, past or future. They understood that prophecy was a call to return to God in

the present tense of the prophet's voice. The prophet proclaims in relation to the future, reflecting a future state of being in the present. Early Christians came to understand the narrative of Christ's salvation as a living road map for their internal being. Within their worldview, what had formerly been the ontological reality of the world was no longer of value. They were changed, and the world was changed whether it was aware of it or not. Their attempt to understand the narrative and its meaning was to recreate the story of Christ's life, sacrifice, and resurrection again and again, to live it out as though it were happening each time they chose to re-enact it. The earliest Christians rather quickly came to understand that this was how they could live out the commandment of Christ to join Him in His resurrected state. The Divine Liturgy was and still is the Parousia, the end, the experience of the heavenly Jerusalem descending to accept the believing populace left upon the earth along with those who are already in heaven praising and worshipping God. It is the eschaton realized.

Believing that the end was immanent in the beginning of their new faith, there was no longer a coherent system of cause and effect for Orthodox Christians; there was only the coming of the One who would liberate them from suffering and grant them everlasting life.

They actively sought to dwell within a world beyond the end of things, hastening that end so that they might pass through to the other side of the eschaton's telos. To accomplish this, they set about to simulate the eschaton in the liturgical life of the church. Thus the Divine Liturgy of the Orthodox Church is to this day a temporal simulacrum in this world of the eternal reality of the next world.

We hope that this translation begins to bring to Western sensibilities the inherent "in-breaking" of Christ's presence in which the earliest Christians believed and for which they prayed, for which they witnessed and gave their lives. The "simulation" of the heaven on earth that is the Divine Liturgy was real and true to them; the map was as much the truth as the geography it represented. This is still true today for Orthodox Christians, and it is our desire for the *Apocalypse* to be understood, even experientially apprehended in this fullness of human experience and metanarrative urgency.

The publisher hopes that this translation, a new interpretation into English of the *Apocalypse*, opens the door to a re-examination of the *Apocalypse*'s true intention. The publisher also hopes that it will become a matter of intense discussion, among a wide variety of

those who call themselves "believers," whether the contemporary Western sense of apocalyptic doom that infuses the culture can be seen for what it is: a result of a gross misreading of the *Apocalypse*'s true meaning.

The Christ-believing Christians will most assuredly understand the earnest hope of our attempt to bring a fresh and honest meaning to the text in English. Those whose interest is intellectual will at the very least glean a glimpse of the believer's intense sensate beliefs. For those who believe that the text is more important than the subject to which it points, they will have one more object against which to measure the futility of their frustrations when the world continues to thwart their perceptions of their own transformations.

Feast of the
Transfiguration, 2002

Father Philemon D. Sevastiades
Duluth and New York

Acknowledgments

As for those to whom thanks could only begin to embrace the rich and varied gifts they have given me, I cannot begin to list them adequately here. For the many of you who have been good friends, better than I could be in return, I thank you one and all.

On this occasion, I wish to thank Columbia University's Department of Religion for they instilled in me a sense of warmth and joy for a life in the mind. I especially wish to thank Prof. Randall Balmer and Prof. Jeffrey Perl, now at Duke University, the former for our continuing friendship and the latter for his deep and abiding influence upon my thinking. Every warning he gave about the Academy is precisely true. As for making an historian interested in the importance of textual studies and their relationship to the development of history, I must acknowledge Prof. Holland Hendrix, former President of Union Theological Seminary.

I wish to thank John and Anne Mavroudis for their continuing support and vision. They are servants of the Lord, and manage to accomplish this difficult task while always being of good cheer and generosity.

I wish to thank His Eminence Archbishop Spyridon, whose faith in finding new, contemporary ways to bring the light of Orthodox Christianity into the view of the

West was and is unequalled and uncompromising in its honesty.

Thanks must go to my good friend, my brother in Christ, my colleague and my brother in spirit, Mark Arey. We have lived through lifetimes of pressure, grief, joy and accomplishment.

Patra McSharry Sevastiades is the touchstone from which I gather my wits and clarity in this world. Her talents are as brilliant as her love, her mind as clear and comforting as her heart is genuine.

Had my mother Evangeline Weiss lived to see this work, I know that she would have shared in the joy with her usual quiet pride. She, together with my father, gave me everything and more that I needed for many years, to make this possible.

Finally, for me this work is in memory of the two men who were pillars in my life. Their numerous gifts both measurable and immeasurable bear the image of their loving presence in my life and will do so always. For my father, Dr. Bernard Demetrius Weiss, and my Spiritual Father, the Rev. Protopresbyter Basil Gregory— this is because of you.

TRANSLATOR'S NOTE

"All Scripture is inspired by God . . ."   —II Timothy 3:16

To translate a text is above all else to serve a text, to convey as best as possible the meaning of the original, or as St. Jerome put it, "to express not word for word, but meaning for meaning."

A translator serves the original text in the same way an illuminator serves a manuscript—by bringing meaning to light and light to meaning. Instead of using marginal images, glosses, and ornamental flourishes served up in brilliant colors, a translator chooses words, phrases, expressions, idioms, punctuation—a host of "word-images"—to interpret the original. To transpose a sentence of Susan Sontag, the task of translation is virtually one of interpretation. When translating Sacred Scripture, this process should allow the original inspired text to become "luminous for its truth" (Eric Voegelin). Indeed, recognizing that a translation can never be considered "inspired," there is all the more need for the translated words—the Message—to be illuminated by the translator.

The *Apocalypse* is a powerful visionary text, a prophetic explosion. As the final vision and statement of

the New Testament, it presents itself to every generation with a story that may defy any one interpretation, but not our imagination. The text is a vibrant, pulsing word-image, streaked often with violent colorations, bathed at other times in deeply peaceful hues. Here we truly have text as image. In the Orthodox Christian Church, images (or icons, as they are called) can serve as text. An icon tells a story, often conflating time and collapsing discrete narratives into a single image with multiple references.

In the word-images of Sacred Scripture, and particularly in the *Apocalypse*, the words project onto the mind and spirit a vibrant, visual feast. Of themselves, the words are scratches on a page, but the symbolic content of these alphabetic characters and their presentation on the page inform the reader with a narrative of truly cosmic proportions. Sacred Text compels a translator constantly to re-image the meaning of these symbols; translation is achieved when one finally lets go of the process and allows the Message to be conveyed in another set of symbolic scratches. The translator renders service to the text when he or she re-images the original word-images in another language, not re-imagines them! That is why a "good" translation will always have the feel of a palimpsest: a manuscript from which the original writing

has been effaced so that other writing can be superimposed, but that still bears traces of its original text.

The present translation strives to reflect the theology of Ancient and Undivided Christianity as contained in the Nicene Creed of the Orthodox Christian Church, i.e., the theology of its first hearers, the theology from which all Christianity, East and West, originally sprang. It is a translation based on sound and based on voice. It is a translation that is meant to be heard, as it was by the ancient Christians, for "faith cometh by hearing."

This work is a translation of the *Apokalypsis Ioannou* from the 1904 authorized edition of the Greek New Testament of the Orthodox Christian Church, *Ē Kainē Diathēkē engrisei tēs Megalēs tou Christou Ekklēsias*. The 1904 edition was published by the Ecumenical Patriarchate of Constantinople and thus could rightly be called a "Textus Constantinopolitanus." No autographs of any portion of Sacred Scripture exist, and the search for the original archetype, the so-called "urtext," is an increasingly controversial endeavor. The Millennium Translation Project selected this particular Greek edition of the New Testament because it is based on the liturgy and communal prayers of the most ancient—and, some would say, the most authentic—Christian community. Renowned textual scholar Bruce

M. Metzger, in describing the text, writes:

> Under the editorial supervision of Professor B.
> Antoniades and issued by the authority of the
> Ecumenical Patriarchate of the Orthodox Church,
> the edition is based on about sixty lectionaries dat-
> ing from the ninth to the sixteenth centuries. Those
> portions of the New Testament that are not con-
> tained in lectionaries (in addition to the Book of
> Revelation in its entirety, certain parts of Acts not
> read in the church) are based on continuous text
> Byzantine manuscripts, mostly cursive and later
> than the tenth century.[1]

Thus the Textus Constantinopolitanus is the living
text of a living, praying, worshipping Church. It is based
on the ancient ecclesiastical tradition of the Great Church
of Christ of Constantinople that embodies the continuous
memory of the Orthodox Christian Church. The preface
of the 1904 edition speaks of this text as being constructed
"not on the basis of the codices written in uncials that are
being employed for *critical editions*, but on the basis of
those manuscripts that have usually been overlooked and
that 'have been rejected by the builders,' according to the
Scriptural saying" (emphasis added). It is a text that bears
the official sanction (*egkrisis*) of the Church, which is more

---

[1] Bruce M. Metzger, "Greek Lectionaries and a Critical Edition of the Greek New
Testament," in *Die Alten Übersetzungen des Neuen Testaments, Die Kirchenväterzitate und
Lektionare*, ed. K. Aland (Berlin: Walter De Gruyter, 1972), p. 486.

than an imprimatur. This text is the living witness of the memory of the Church, which rests on the promise of Jesus Christ, Who said:

> "I have spoken these things to you while I yet abide with you. But the Paraclete, the Holy Spirit, Whom the Father will send in My Name, He is the One Who will teach you all things, and bring into your memory all the things I have told you." (John 14:25–26)

By design, Textus Constantinopolitanus is not, nor was it intended to be, a critical text. And so it is no surprise that Metzger's assessment is that "for scientific purposes, the Antoniades edition leaves much to be desired."[2] But elsewhere, Metzger himself affirms the value of lectionary texts: "since they are liturgical books, it is probable that they would be conservative in transmitting an older and more traditional type of text than the date of the copying of a given lectionary manuscript might suggest would be the case."[3] Noted authority Kenneth W. Clark echoes this point of view:

> It is generally held, furthermore, that public reading of the lectionary text tended to stereotype it and remove it from the centrifugal forces that shattered the unity of the witnesses. Therefore, the

[2]Ibid., p. 486.
[3]Ibid., p. 479.

lectionary text would be a conservative text and once understood, should bear valuable witness to the text in the early period of the Church.[4]

Thus the Constantinopolitan Text is the living text of a living Church, a Church that still worships in the original language of the New Testament. To this day, more than one-third of all manuscripts of the New Testament remain in Greece, and more than one-third of those manuscripts are housed in the monasteries of Mount Athos, which is still under the spiritual care of the Ecumenical Patriarchate of Constantinople.

Finally, in translating Sacred Scripture, the choice of punctuation and capitalization is a decision of the translator and/or editor. The earliest Greek texts do not possess these grammatical distinctions, not even versification. However, in order to facilitate comparison, all editorial and grammatical decisions have been made within the constraints of chapter and verse numbering consistent with the King James Version.

Needless to say, this translation would not have come about without the remarkable energies and support of many people. Chief among them are John and Anne Mavroudis, whose undaunted faith and generosity have

---

[4]Kenneth W. Clark, "The Background of the New Testament and Its Eschatology," in *The Effect of Textual Criticism upon New Testament Studies. Essays in Honour of Charles Harold Dodd*, ed. W. D. Davies and D. Daube (Cambridge, 1956), p. 46.

made this translation possible. Many thanks go as well to Leo and Evanthia Condakes and Michael and Anastasia Cantonis, for their financial assistance to the publication.

His Eminence Archbishop Spyridon is owed a debt of gratitude for his counsel on the Textus Constantinopolitanus. A posthumous thanks is owed to my mentor in the Classics, the late Professor William Turner Avery, who taught me everything I needed to know about translating twenty-five years before I knew how to use it.

Penultimately, to my collaborators, the publisher, Father Philemon Sevastiades and the editor, Patra McSharry Sevastiades . . . What is good in this translation would not have been possible without them both. Patra wove the words together with artistry beyond my means.

Finally, to my mother, Anne, and my brothers, Christopher and Stephen. Their belief in me has always surpassed my deservedness.

And as for my beloved and late father, Herbert Littleton Arey, this translation is for him. He never had the opportunity to read the text. But he is living it now. May his memory be eternal.

"Happy and blessed are the dead, who die in the Lord at this time." –Revelation 14:13

Pentecost 2002   Mark B. Arey
                                                              New York

APOCALYPSE
THE BOOK OF REVELATION

CHAPTER ONE

The Apocalypse of Jesus Christ, given to Him by God to reveal unto His servants the future events that must soon unfold. Indeed, He sent signs through His Angelic Messenger to His servant John, ^{1:2)} who declared his faith in God's word and in the testament of Jesus Christ, bearing witness to all that he saw. ^{1:3)} Blessed is the one who reads and all who listen to the words of this prophecy and diligently observe everything written in it. Truly, its moment is fast approaching!

^{1:4)} John, to the seven Churches that are in Asia Minor: Grace and peace be to you from God, Who Is and Was and Is To Come, and from the Seven Spirits that are before His throne: ^{1:5)} and grace and peace from Jesus Christ, the Faithful Witness, the First-born from the dead, the

Sovereign of the kings of the earth, Who loved us and washed us clean from our sins by His own Blood 1:6) and established us as a Kingdom, making us priests of God His Father. Glory and dominion to Him unto ages of ages! Amen!

1:7) Behold! He is coming on the clouds, and every eye will see Him, even those who pierced Him, and all the peoples of the earth will howl and wail. Yes! Amen!

1:8) "I Am[1] the **A**lpha and the **Ω**mega, Who Is and Was and Is To Come, the Pantokrator—the Ruler of All!" The Lord God speaks!

1:9) I, John—your brother and your companion in tribulation, in the Kingdom, and in the patient waiting for Jesus Christ—was banished to the island that is called Patmos, on account of God's word and the testament of Jesus Christ.

1:10) It was a Sunday, the Lord's Day, and I was enraptured in spirit. Then I heard a blaring sound behind me like a trumpet 1:11) that said, "Write down on a scroll what you see and send it to the seven Churches: to Ephesus and Smyrna, to Pergamon and Thyateira, to Sardis and Philadelpheia, and to Laodiceia."

---

[1]This capitalization ("I Am") is used throughout to translate the Greek *ego eimi*, which, in the writings of the Apostle John, signifies the Divine Name, the "O ΩN" (the LXX translation of the Tetragrammaton, "YHWH"), revealed by God to Moses at the Burning Bush (Exodus 3:14, LXX), often translated, "I AM WHO I AM."

1:12) I turned to see whose voice was speaking to me. And when I turned, I saw seven golden lampstands. 1:13) In the midst of the seven lampstands was One Whose likeness was as the Son of Man. He was robed with a garment that flowed down to His feet; fastened across His breast was a golden sash. 1:14) His head and hair were white, like white wool, as white as snow, and His eyes flashed like fiery flames. 1:15) His feet were like molten brass come fresh out of a fiery furnace—red hot and glowing, and the sound of His voice was like the surge of mighty waters. 1:16) In His right hand He held seven stars; and from His mouth came forth a razor-swift, dazzling double-edged sword. His countenance blazed like the sun, shining in all its brilliant power.

1:17) When I saw Him, I collapsed at His feet like one dead. But He laid His right hand upon me and said, "Fear not! I Am the First and the Last. 1:18) I am He Who lives, dead though I was, and behold! I am alive forever! And I possess the keys of Death and of Hades. 1:19) So now, write down everything you have seen: the things that are now and the things that will take place hereafter. 1:20) The mystery of the seven stars that you saw upon My right hand is this: the seven stars are the Angelic Messengers of the seven Churches. The mystery of the seven golden lampstands is this: the seven lampstands are the seven Churches."

CHAPTER TWO

"**U**nto the Angel of the Church in Ephesus, write: 'Thus says the One Who holds the seven stars in His right hand, Who walks amidst the seven golden lampstands. ^{2:2)} I know your deeds, your toil, and your patience, and that you have never tolerated the wicked. You have put to the test those who claim to be apostles, and are not! You have proven that they were liars. ^{2:3)} For the sake of My Name you have endured patiently, stood your ground, and have not wearied.

^{2:4)} "'But I have this against you: that you have deserted your first love. ^{2:5)} Therefore, remember how far away you have fallen. Return repentant, and perform your first works again. If not, I will come quickly, and, unless you repent, I will take your lampstand from its place.

2:6) "'But you do have this: you hate the deeds of the Nicolaitans, which I despise. 2:7) You who have ears to hear, listen to what the Spirit speaks to the Churches. I will bestow upon the victor the gift of eating from the Tree of Life, which stands in the midst of the Paradise of My God.'

2:8) "And unto the Angel of the Church in Smyrna, write: 'Thus says the First and the Last, He Who was dead and now is alive. 2:9) I know your deeds, your tribulation and your poverty (but in truth your cup runs over). And I am aware of the blasphemy of those who call themselves "Jews" (and are not!), but who are in reality the assembly of Satan.

2:10) "'Do not be afraid of what you are about to suffer. Behold! Even now the Devil is ready to cast some of you into prison and torture you. You must endure this trial for ten days. Be faithful even unto death, and I will give you a crown of life! 2:11) You who have ears to hear, listen to what the Spirit speaks to the Churches. The overcomer will not be harmed by the second death.'

2:12) "And unto the Angel of the Church in Pergamon, write: 'Thus says the One Who possesses the razor-swift, dazzling double-edged sword. 2:13) I know your deeds and how you have held fast to My Name. Even though you live in the shadow of Satan's throne, you have not

denied your faith in Me—even during the days when My faithful witness Antipas was executed before your very eyes, in Satan's own domain!

2:14) "'Nevertheless, I have a few things against you. You still have in your midst those who cling to the doctrine of Balaam—the same Balaam who taught Balak to throw a stumbling-block before the Children of Israel, to eat food sacrificed to idols, and to commit immoral acts. 2:15) So you see, even you have some who have been indoctrinated by the Nicolaitans.

2:16) "'Repent! Turn back! If not, I will come swiftly and strike them with the sword that is in My mouth. 2:17) You who have ears to hear, listen to what the Spirit speaks to the Churches. My gifts to the victor will be a white writ of acquittal and to partake of the secret hidden manna. Upon the writ will be a new name, which only the one who receives it knows.'

2:18) "And unto the Angel of the Church in Thyateira, write: 'Thus says the Son of God, Whose eyes flash like fiery flames, and Whose feet are like molten brass. 2:19) I know your deeds and your love, your devotion to serving others, your faith, and your endurance. Indeed, your works of late far surpass your early works.

2:20) "'Still, I have a few things against you. You consented to have the woman, Jezebel (who calls herself a

"prophetess"), as a teacher among you. She beguiles my servants and tricks them into grievous immorality and the defilement of eating food sacrificed to idols. 2:21) Indeed, I gave this woman time to repent and change her ways, but she was unwilling to repent of her immorality. 2:22) Behold! I will hurl her onto a bed of pain and sickness; and I will throw those who have committed adultery with her into deep distress, unless they repent of their deeds. 2:23) And I will consign her offspring to death. All the Churches will know that I Am He Who searches out the innermost core of thought and intention, and that I will render to each of you according to your deeds.

2:24) "'Now, I say to all the rest of you in Thyateira (all those who have not been swayed by her propaganda, who have not known the "depths of Satan," as they themselves put it), I place upon you no other burden than this: 2:25) Hold on to what you have until I return! 2:26) To the one who overcomes and perseveres in My deeds until the end, I will give authority over the Nations. 2:27) You will shepherd them with a rod of iron such as would shatter the clay vessels of a potter, even as I received from My Father. 2:28) And I will give you the morning star. 2:29) You who have ears to hear, listen to what the Spirit speaks to the Churches.'"

CHAPTER THREE

"**U**nto the Angel of the Church in Sardis, write: 'Thus says the One Who possesses the Seven Spirits of God and the seven stars. I know your deeds—that you are renowned for your dynamism and vitality; but you are dead! ^{3:2)} Wake up! Be vigilant! Hold fast to what little remains, or it too will wither and die, for I have found your deeds to be vain and empty in the sight of My God. ^{3:3)} Therefore, recall how you first heard and received the word. Heed it, and repent! For if you do not awaken, I will come upon you like a thief! And you will not know at what moment I will spring upon you.

^{3:4)} "'Yet you still have a few names in Sardis whose garments have not been sullied. They are worthy to walk with Me, arrayed in robes luminous, of purest white.

3:5) Those who conquer will be clothed in robes of light. I will not blot out their names from the Book of Life; rather, I will confess their names and claim them in the presence of My Father and His Angels. 3:6) You who have ears to hear, listen to what the Spirit says to the Churches.'

3:7) "And unto the Angel of the Church in Philadelpheia, write: 'Thus says He Who is Holy and True, Who possesses the key of David—Who opens and there is none who can close, Who closes and there is none who can open. 3:8) I know your deeds! Behold! I did put an open door before you, which no one can close, because you still have a little strength, and you have kept My message intact and have not denied My Name. 3:9) Behold! I will deliver into your hands those of the assembly of Satan (who call themselves "Jews" but in reality are liars). I will make them come and bow down before your feet; and they will know that I have loved you. 3:10) Because you have persevered in My message of patience, I will preserve you from the hour of trial that is about to come upon the whole world—the ordeal for all those who dwell on earth.

3:11) "'I am coming with great haste! Hold on to what you have! See that no one wrests away your crown! 3:12) I will make the victor a pillar in the temple of My God, fixed and immovable, one upon which I will inscribe the

11

Name of My God, and My own new Name, and the Name of the City of My God—the New Jerusalem, which will descend from My God out of Heaven. ^{3:13)} You who have ears to hear, listen to what the Spirit is saying to the Churches.'

^{3:14)} "Unto the Angel of the Church in Laodiceia, write: 'Thus says the AMEN, the Witness Faithful and True, the Origin of God's creation. ^{3:15)} I know your deeds, and that you are neither hot nor cold. O, if only you were either hot or cold! ^{3:16)} But because you are merely lukewarm—neither the one nor the other—I will spit you out of My mouth.

^{3:17)} "'You say: "I need nothing, for I am filthy rich—gorged with riches!" If only you knew how wretched and pitiful, destitute, blind, and naked you are! ^{3:18)} Have I not counseled you to come to Me and acquire the gold refined and purified by fire? Let your riches be this gold! And buy white linen—fair and pure—to be clothed and to cover the embarrassment of your nakedness. And purchase balm that your eyes may be healed, that you may see and understand. ^{3:19)} For as many as I love, I convince and correct, as you would your own child. Therefore, be more fervent to repent.

^{3:20)} "'Behold! I stand at the door and knock. If any of you hears My voice and opens the door, I will come in to

you and recline at table and sup with you, and you with Me. ^{3:21)} My gift will be to enthrone the conqueror beside Me, just as I was a conqueror and was enthroned beside My Father. ^{3:22)} You who have ears to hear, listen to what the Spirit says to the Churches.'"

CHAPTER FOUR

After this I looked up, and behold! A portal opened in Heaven. And I heard the first voice—the one like a trumpet—say to me, "Come up here, and I will show you what must happen in the future."

4:2) Suddenly, I was in the spirit. And behold! A throne stood squarely in the midst of Heaven, with One seated on the throne. 4:3) The One Who sat on the throne was like an epiphany of jasper and sardius—deep translucent bloodstones both; and from all around His throne shone an emerald rainbow. 4:4) Twenty-four thrones encircled His throne, and upon those thrones I saw Twenty-four Presbyters[2] adorned in brilliant shining robes, a crown of gold upon the head of each.

---

[2] Greek *presbyteros*, which can also be translated "elder" (but without a designation of physical age). The word is the root of the English word "priest."

4:5) Thunder, lightning, and voices came forth from the throne, and seven lamps of fire burned before it—the Seven Spirits of God!

4:6) A sea of glass—an ocean of crystal—expanded before the throne. Within the throne and around the throne were Four Living Beings teeming with eyes. 4:7) The first Being was like a lion, the second Being was like a young bull, the third Being bore the face of a person, and the fourth Being was like an eagle on the wing. 4:8) Each of the Four Living Beings was brimming with eyes within and without and possessed six wings. They never took any rest, but night and day chanted, "Holy! Holy! Holy! Lord God, Pantokrator—Ruler of All—Who Was and Is and Is To Come!"

4:9) When the Living Beings offered up these songs of glory, honor, and thanksgiving to the One seated on the throne, Who lives for all eternity, 4:10) the Twenty-four Presbyters fell prostrate before Him. They cast their crowns before His throne and worshipped Him Who lives for all eternity, singing, 4:11) "Worthy are You, O Lord, to receive glory, honor, and power, for You fashioned everything that is, and by Your will everything exists and has been created!"

CHAPTER FIVE

Then I looked and saw that in the right hand of the One seated on the throne was a scroll with writing all over—inside and out—sealed with seven seals. 5:2) And I saw a mighty Angelic Herald proclaim with his colossal voice, "Is there anyone who can open the scroll and break its seals?" 5:3) And no one, neither in Heaven, nor on earth, nor below the earth, was able to open the scroll, or even to look upon it. 5:4) Then I began to weep uncontrollably, for no one could be found who was worthy enough to open the scroll, or even to look upon it.

5:5) "Dry your tears," one of the Presbyters said to me. "Behold! the Lion of the tribe of Judah—the Root of David! He has triumphed and can break open the scroll and its seven seals!"

^{5:6)} And I saw in the midst of the throne, in the midst of the Four Living Beings, in the midst of the Presbyters—a Lamb, standing upright, bearing the wounds of His own sacrifice. He had seven horns and seven eyes, which are the Seven Spirits of God sent out over all the earth. ^{5:7)} And the Lamb came forward and claimed the scroll from the right hand of the One seated on the throne.

^{5:8)} When the Lamb took hold of the scroll, the Four Living Beings and the Twenty-four Presbyters fell on their faces before Him. Each one had a lyre and a vial made from pure gold, overflowing with thick fumes of incense, which are the prayers of the Saints. ^{5:9)} And they erupted in chant, glorious and new: "Worthy are You to receive the scroll and to open its seals, for You were the Sacrifice, and You have redeemed us unto God with Your own Blood—from every tribe and tongue, every people and nation, ^{5:10)} making them kings and priests for our God, to reign over the earth."

^{5:11)} Then I looked, and I heard the sound of multitudes of Angels round about the throne, together with the Living Beings and the Presbyters, and the number of Angels must have been thousands upon thousands, even ten thousand times ten thousand. ^{5:12)} They cried out with a loud voice, "Worthy is the Lamb Who was

sacrificed to receive power and abundance and wisdom and strength and honor and glory and blessing!"

5:13) And then I heard every single thing that is alive—in Heaven, on the earth, below the earth, in the oceans—everything everywhere!—lift up their voices and cry aloud, "To the One seated on the throne and to the Lamb, blessing and honor and glory and dominion unto ages of ages!"

5:14) "Amen!" pronounced the Four Living Beings, and the Twenty-four Presbyters fell prostrate in worship.

CHAPTER SIX

Then I saw the Lamb crack open[3] the first of the seven seals. And I heard the voice of the first Living Being (the one like a lion), as a peal of thunder, roar, "Come!" 6:2) And I looked, and behold! A white horse! The horse's rider brandished an archer's bow and was granted a crown. He rode out triumphantly on his way to conquer.

6:3) When the Lamb shattered the second seal, I heard the second Living Being (the one like a young bull) bellow forth, "Come!" 6:4) And another horse, red like a raging fire! Its rider was given a great sword. He was allowed to pluck peace from the earth, so that a rampage of killing raged.

---

[3] Ancient seals were made primarily of lead and had to be broken in order to be opened.

^{6:5)} When the Lamb broke open the third seal, I heard the third Living Being (the one with a human face) command, "Come!" And I looked, and behold! Another horse, black as pitch! Its rider held the yoked scales of a balance in his hand. ^{6:6)} Then I heard a sound like a voice in the midst of the Four Living Beings that said, "A ration of wheat for your silver, three rations of barley for the same; but damage not the olive oil or the wine."

^{6:7)} When the Lamb fractured the fourth seal, I heard the fourth Living Being (the one like an eagle) cry out, "Come!" ^{6:8)} And I looked, and behold! A greenish mucus-colored horse! Its rider's name was Death, and Hades followed close on his heels. Authority was given to them over one quarter of the earth. Their killing spree went on and on, fueled by the sword, by famine, by pestilent death, and by the wild animals of the earth.

^{6:9)} When the Lamb broke the fifth seal, I looked at the altar of sacrifice and saw beneath it the souls of all those who had been slaughtered for the word of God and on account of their martyr's witness for the Lamb. ^{6:10)} A deafening outcry swelled from them, saying, "How long, O Master, Holy and True, until You judge those who dwell on earth and vindicate our blood?"

^{6:11)} Then a shining white robe was given to each of them. They were told to rest a little while longer, until the

time when their brothers and sisters, their fellow servants, would be murdered, even as they had been, fulfilling the number of the Martyrs.

6:12) Then I saw the Lamb fragment the sixth seal, and an immense quake shook the earth. The sun became sooty, as black as sackcloth, and the moon turned to blood. 6:13) The stars fell from the sky and crashed into the earth, like the unripe fruit of a fig tree when shaken by a gust of wind. 6:14) Heaven itself recoiled like a tightly wound scroll, and every mountain and island heaved and shook.

6:15) Then the kings and counselors of the earth— monarchs, majesties, magnates all—the powerful, together with every slave and every freeman, hid in the caves and clefts of the mountains, 6:16) and called out to the mountains and to the rocks, "Fall on us! Hide us from the presence of the One seated on the throne and from the wrath of the Lamb! 6:17) For the awesome day of His wrath has come, and who can withstand it?"

CHAPTER SEVEN

After this, I saw four Angels standing at the four corners of the earth, holding back the four winds. The air grew still; the sea breezes ceased; not a single tree rustled. 7:2) And I saw another Angel ascend from the dawning sun, bearing the seal of the Living God. He cried out with a loud voice to the four Angels, who were allowed to afflict both land and sea, 7:3) "Touch not the land or the waters, or the trees, until we have put the seal of our God upon the foreheads of His servants."

7:4) Then I heard the number, the number of those to be sealed—144,000—from every tribe of the Sons of Israel: 7:5) from the tribe of Judah, 12,000 sealed; from the tribe of Rouben, 12,000 sealed; from the tribe of Gad, 12,000 sealed; 7:6) from the tribe of Aser, 12,000 sealed; from the

tribe of Nephthaleim, 12,000 sealed; from the tribe of Manasses, 12,000 sealed; 7:7) from the tribe of Symeon, 12,000 sealed; from the tribe of Levi, 12,000 sealed; from the tribe of Issachar, 12,000 sealed; 7:8) from the tribe of Zaboulon, 12,000 sealed; from the tribe of Joseph, 12,000 sealed; from the tribe of Benjamin, 12,000 sealed.

7:9) Then I looked and saw wave upon wave of humanity, so many that no one could count them, from every nation, tribe, race, and language, all standing before the throne and before the Lamb. They were arrayed in brilliant white and held palm branches in their hands. 7:10) And their cry was a tremendous shout: "Salvation by our God Enthroned and by the Lamb!"

7:11) Then all the Angels gathered around the throne and around the Presbyters and the Four Living Beings, and they all fell down upon their faces before the throne and worshipped God, 7:12) singing, "Amen! Blessing and glory and wisdom and thanksgiving and honor and power and strength to our God unto ages of ages. Amen!"

7:13) Then one of the Presbyters addressed me and asked, "Do you know those people arrayed in the white robes? Do you know from where they have come?"

7:14) "My lord, you know," I answered him.

"These are the ones who have passed through the Great Tribulation," he said to me. "They have washed

their robes clean in the Blood of the Lamb, making them shine glistening white. 7:15) Therefore, they are now before the throne of God. Day and night they offer their praise and adoration to Him in His temple. The One seated on the throne will make His tabernacle among them. 7:16) They will hunger and thirst no more, neither suffer the burning heat of the sun, 7:17) for the Lamb in the midst of the throne shepherds them, and He will guide them to fountains flowing with the water of life. And God will wipe away every tear from their eyes."

CHAPTER EIGHT

When the Lamb opened the seventh seal, there was silence in Heaven for half an hour.

8:2) Then I saw the seven Angels who stand before God, and seven trumpets were given to them.

8:3) Another Angel came, and he stood before the altar of sacrifice. He had a censer of pure gold. He was given a great quantity of incense, and he began to offer it with the prayers of all the Saints on the golden altar before the throne. 8:4) A smoky cloud of incense, with the prayers of the Saints, ascended from the hand of the Angel into the presence of God. 8:5) Then the Angel took the censer, filled it to the brim with fire from the altar of sacrifice, and hurled the fire to earth. Explosions boomed—a clap of thunder, a flash of lightning, and the quaking of the earth!

8:6) And the seven Angels readied themselves to sound their seven trumpets.

8:7) When the first Angel blasted his trumpet, a storm of hail and fire mixed with blood was launched to earth, scorching a third of the earth. Fire consumed a third of all the trees, and all the young green grass was incinerated.

8:8) When the second Angel sounded his trumpet, a towering mountain, burning with fire, was cast into the sea, and a third part of the sea became blood. 8:9) A third of the sea creatures (those with the life force) died, and a third of all ships were utterly destroyed.

8:10) When the third Angel let forth the peal of his trumpet, a great star burning like a brilliant torch plummeted from the sky. It crashed into a third of the rivers and the sources of all fresh water. 8:11) And the name of the star was "Absinthe." A third of all the fresh water was poisoned (as if contaminated with absinthe), and many people perished from that water.

8:12) When the fourth Angel's trumpet roared, a third portion of the sun, a third portion of the moon, and a third portion of the stars were blotted out, so that a third of each was overwhelmed by darkness. The day was shortened by a third, and likewise the night was deprived of a third of its lesser lights.

8:13) Then I looked: An eagle was flying at the summit of Heaven. "Woe! Woe! Woe to all the inhabitants of the earth!" I heard his voice thunder. "For there are yet three trumpets to be sounded by three Angels to come!"

CHAPTER NINE

When the fifth Angel blew his trumpet, I saw a star rocketing from Heaven toward the earth, and he was given the key to the pit of the abyss. ^{9:2)} He unlocked the pit of the abyss, and smoke spewed from the pit as from a raging furnace. The smoke that poured forth from the pit obscured the sun, filling the air with darkness.

^{9:3)} Then locusts surged from the smoke, filled with the power of the scorpions that scour the earth. ^{9:4)} The locusts were instructed not to damage the earth's vegetation—no green plant, no tree—but to torment only the people who did not have the seal of God on their foreheads. ^{9:5)} They were not permitted to kill them, only to scourge them for five months. Their sting was like that of a scorpion when it strikes. ^{9:6)} In those days people will

seek to die, but they will find no release. They will beg to die, but death will elude them.

9:7) The locusts look like horses armed to the teeth for battle. On their heads are crowns that appear to be of gold. Their faces resemble human faces. 9:8) Their hair is like the hair of a woman, and their teeth are like the fangs of a lion. 9:9) They have iron-like breastplates, and the sound of their wings is like the stampede of horses' hooves when chariots charge into battle. 9:10) They have tails resembling scorpion tails, tails loaded with stingers. They possess a brute force to torment humankind for five months. 9:11) A king rules over them, the Angel of the abyss, whose name in Hebrew is "Abaddon," but in Greek, "Apollyon."[4]

9:12) One woe is past. Behold! Two more woes are yet to come!

9:13) When the sixth Angel sounded his trumpet, I heard a voice coming from the four horns on the golden altar of sacrifice that stands before God. 9:14) And the voice said to the sixth Angel who had just blown his trumpet, "Let loose the four Angels who have been bound at the great river Euphrates." 9:15) Then the four Angels, who had been prepared for that very hour, that very day, that very month and year, were unleashed to eradicate a third of humankind.

---

[4] Literally, "The Destroyer," cf. Exodus 12:23.

9:16) And I heard the roar of the number of their host, a cavalry of 20,000 myriads: 200 million! 9:17) This is how I saw those horses and their riders in my vision. The horses had armored breastplates that burned with bloody purple flames of sulphur. Their heads seemed like the heads of lions, and they exhaled fire, smoke, and brimstone. 9:18) These three plagues—the fire, the smoke, and the brimstone that poured from the horses' mouths—annihilated a third of all humankind. 9:19) Indeed, each horse's force was in its mouth and in its tail, and their tails were like snakes with heads, and the head of each was bent on mayhem.

9:20) Yet that which was left of humankind, which was not obliterated by these pernicious scourges, did not turn from their evil deeds. They persisted in worshipping demons—idols of gold, silver, bronze, stone, and wood, which cannot see, cannot hear, cannot walk. 9:21) And they did not repent of their murders, or of their occult practices, or of their immorality, or of their thievery.

CHAPTER TEN

Then I saw another mighty Angel descending from Heaven, draped with clouds and with a rainbow about his head. His face shone like the sun, and his legs down to his feet were like pillars of fire. ^{10:2)} He alighted with his right foot on the surface of the sea and his left foot on the land. In his hand he held an open scroll.[5] ^{10:3)} He roared like a lion, and when he did, seven peals of thunder answered him. ^{10:4)} I was about to write down what the seven thunders said, when I heard a voice from Heaven: "Seal up what the seven thunders divulged; write it not!"

^{10:5)} Then the Angel whom I had seen straddling land and sea stretched forth his right hand toward Heaven

---

[5]Greek, *biblion*; Textus Receptus and Textus Criticus have *biblaridion,* "little scroll."

^{10:6)} and swore by Him Who lives for all eternity, Who created Heaven and everything therein, the earth and everything therein, and the sea and everything therein, "No more time! ^{10:7)} But on the day when the seventh Angel is poised to sound his trumpet,⁶ then will the mystery of God be fulfilled, as He declared to His servants, the Prophets—in the Good News of the Gospel!"

^{10:8)} And the same voice that I had heard from Heaven spoke to me again and said, "Go, take the small open scroll from the hand of the Angel who stands astride both land and sea." ^{10:9)} So I approached the Angel and told him to give the little scroll to me.

"Take it," he said to me, "and swallow it. It will taste as sweet as honey in your mouth, but it will sour your stomach." ^{10:10)} So I took the scroll from the hand of the Angel and ate it. It was as he said, sweet as honey in my mouth and bitter in my stomach. ^{10:11)} Then he said to me, "You must prophesy yet again for peoples, nations, tongues, and many kings."

---

⁶Verse 11:15.

CHAPTER ELEVEN

Then the Angel gave me a reed that was as straight as a rod, saying, "Arise and measure the temple of God, and the altar of sacrifice, and those who worship there. 11:2) But avoid the outer courtyard of the temple and do not measure it, for it has been surrendered to the Gentiles, who will trample down the Holy City for forty-two months. 11:3) But I will allow my Two Witnesses to prophesy for 1,260 days clothed in sackcloth. 11:4) They are two olive trees, two lampstands that stand in the presence of the God of the earth. 11:5) Any enemy who desires to harm them will be consumed by the fire that spews forth from their mouths; thus will anyone who tries to hurt them be killed! 11:6) They will have authority to lock up the sky so that no showers will rain down during the days of

their prophecy. And they will have authority over the waters, to transform them into blood. Indeed, whenever they wish they will be able to smite the land with every kind of plague.

11:7) "And when they have completed their testimony, the monster that has clawed up from the abyss will attack them, and overwhelm them, and execute them. 11:8) Their corpses will be flung into the streets of the great city that is called, in an allegorical sense, "Sodom" and "Egypt," where their Lord was crucified. 11:9) And all peoples, tribes, tongues, and nations will look upon their dead bodies for three-and-a-half days, and they will not allow them to be buried. 11:10) The inhabitants of earth will celebrate and revel in their deaths. They will even exchange gifts with one another, because the two prophets, who tested them and proved them guilty, are dead!

11:11) "But after three-and-a-half days, the spirit of life that comes from God will enter into them, and they will stand up. Horror and dread will seize all who see it! 11:12) Then a mighty voice from Heaven will summon them, saying, 'Come up here!' and they will ascend to Heaven in a cloud while their enemies are left gaping at the sight.

11:13) "That same day, a great earthquake will strike, and a tenth of the city will collapse. The toll of the dead from that earthquake will comprise 7,000 names, and the

survivors will shake in terror. Only then will they render majesty to the God of Heaven.

11:14) "The second woe has passed. Behold! The third comes quickly!"

11:15) Then the seventh Angel blared his trumpet. Mighty voices resounded in Heaven, proclaiming, "The kingdom of this world belongs to our Lord and to His Christ! And He shall reign unto ages of ages!"

11:16) And the Twenty-four Presbyters, who sit on their thrones before the throne of God, fell on their faces and worshipped God, 11:17) saying, "We give thanks to You, O Lord God Pantokrator—Ruler of All—Who Is and Was and Is To Come, for You have wielded Your awesome power and reign supreme. 11:18) The Nations were enraged—yet it was You Who vented fury! Now is the time for the Nations to be judged. Now is the time for Your servants to receive their due reward. Now is the time for the Prophets and the Saints who fear Your Name, the least with the greatest, to receive their recompense. Now is the time to destroy those who destroy the earth!"

11:19) Then the temple of God in Heaven was thrown wide open, and the Ark of the Covenant of the Lord appeared in His temple. Lightning flashed, thunder roared, and a crushing hailstorm came crashing down. The earth quaked, and terrible sounds were heard.

CHAPTER TWELVE

Αnd an astonishing sign appeared in Heaven: A Woman clothed with the sun. A crown of twelve stars adorned her head, and the moon rested beneath her feet. 12:2) She was great with child and cried out, groaning in the pain of childbirth.

12:3) Then another sign appeared in Heaven: And behold! A monstrous fiery-red Dragon with seven heads and ten horns, a diadem on each of his seven heads! 12:4) His tail lashed out and swept up a third of the stars in the sky, hurling them down to earth. Then the Dragon crouched before the Woman who was about to give birth. He waited for her to deliver, so that he might devour her Child. 12:5) But when she gave birth to her Child—a Son Who will shepherd all the Nations with a rod of iron—the

Child was taken up to God and to His throne. [12:6] And the Woman fled into the desert, where God had prepared a place for her, to nourish and care for her for 1,260 days.

[12:7] Then war broke out in Heaven! Michael and his Angels clashed with the Dragon. The Dragon and his evil angels fought furiously, [12:8] but did not prevail; and their place was no longer found in Heaven. [12:9] The Dragon was hurled down to earth, his vile angels with him. That decrepit old snake! You know his name: the Devil, Satan—the Deceiver of the whole world.

[12:10] Then I heard a magnificent sound echoing throughout Heaven, "Now is the salvation, the awesome might, and the Kingdom of our God! Now is the authority of His Christ! For now is cast out the accuser of our brothers and sisters, who slandered them before God day and night! [12:11] They conquered him through the Blood of the Lamb and through the word of their own testimony; for they loved not this transient life so much that they would shrink from death.

[12:12] "Therefore, let the heavens and all who dwell in them rejoice! But woe to the inhabitants of the land and the sea: for now the Devil is plunged into your midst, and his anger rages because he realizes that his time is short."

12:13) When the Dragon saw that he had been hurled down to earth, he hunted for the Woman who had delivered her Son. 12:14) But the Woman was provided with two wings of a giant eagle so she might fly away to her refuge in the desert, that she might be nourished for a time, and times, and half a time, out of the serpent's reach. 12:15) Then the serpent spewed forth a torrential flood from its mouth in order to engulf and drown her. 12:16) But the earth came to the aid of the Woman, opening a cavity and swallowing up the river that he had vomited. 12:17) Then the Dragon went wild with rage because of the Woman and set out to attack the rest of her offspring, who persevered in the commandments of God, witnessing to the testimony of Jesus.

CHAPTER THIRTEEN

Then I found myself standing on the seashore.[7] I saw a monster with seven heads and ten horns—the Beast—crawl up out of the sea. On each of his ten horns was a diadem, and on each head were sacrilegious names of blasphemy. [13:2) I can best describe the monster as a leopard, but with the feet of a huge bear and a lion's maw. The Dragon supplied him with his own brute strength, as well as his tyrannical power and dominance.

[13:3) Then I saw that one of his heads had seemingly been murdered, but the mortal wound healed. And the whole world became enchanted by the monster.

---

[7]The treatment of this verse in the Textus Constantinopolitanus differs from that in the Textus Criticus and those translations that depend on it. In those versions, it is positioned as the last verse (18) of the previous chapter, and the verb "to stand" is in the third person singular. Some English translations make the subject of this verb the "Dragon," while others make it the "Beast." Textus Constantinopolitanus agrees with the Textus Receptus, the basis for the King James Version.

13:4) And they began to worship the monster, and on everyone's lips was, "Can anyone compare to the Beast? Can anyone face him in battle?" But thus, they also worshipped the Dragon, from whom the monster had received his powers.

13:5) The Beast was given leave to speak boastful words brimming with blasphemy and to exert his dominance and to wage war for forty-two months. 13:6) Each time he opened his mouth he blasphemed God, reviling His Name and His Tabernacle and all those who dwell in Heaven.

13:7) And the Beast was permitted to wage war against the Saints and to overwhelm them. He secured control over every nation, people, tribe, and race. 13:8) All the world's inhabitants worshipped the Beast—all whose names are not written in the Book of Life of the Lamb, Who was sacrificed from the very foundation of the cosmos.

13:9) If you have ears to hear this, then listen well! 13:10) If you are led away into captivity, into captivity you shall go! If you are to die by the sword, then by the sword you shall surely die! Now here is the patience and the faith of the Saints!

13:11) Then I saw another monster slither up from below the earth. He had two horns like a ram, but he spoke like the Dragon. 13:12) When he was in the presence

of the first monster, he acted with all the powers of the first monster. He was the reason that the whole earth—everyone!—worshipped the first monster, whose mortal wound had reverted. 13:13) This second monster concocted spectacular supernatural phenomena for people to see, such as making fire fall from the sky. 13:14) And he deceived and led astray the world's inhabitants through these prodigious displays that he performed in the presence of the Beast. He even insisted that the people of earth make an idol of the Beast who was mortally wounded with an assassin's dagger, yet lived. 13:15) Indeed, he animated the idol of the Beast so that it could speak. Anyone who would not bow down and worship the idol of the Beast was executed. 13:16) He also forced everyone, small and great, rich and poor, slave and free, to be punctured on the right hand or forehead with a mark (the *charagma*). 13:17) Without this mark, the name of the Beast, or the cipher of his name, no one could buy, sell, or trade.

13:18) Now here is wisdom! If you have spiritual understanding, then calculate the number of the Beast. Indeed, it is the cipher of a man. And the number is 666![8]

---

[8] "666" in Greek letter values is χξστ. In the earliest surviving manuscripts, the words "six hundred sixty-six" are spelled out.

CHAPTER FOURTEEN

Then I looked, and behold! The Lamb stood upon Mount Sion! One hundred forty-four thousand stood by Him, all with His Name and the Name of His Father inscribed upon their foreheads. 14:2) And I heard a sound from Heaven, like the roar of many waters and the crash of great peals of thunder; and the sound I heard was like the music of harpists strumming their harps. 14:3) They were chanting a new song before the throne, in the presence of the Four Living Beings and the Presbyters; no one could learn their song except the 144,000, who were the redeemed of the earth.

14:4) These 144,000 are virgins, for they have never been seduced, nor have they been seducers. They follow the Lamb wherever He leads. They have been redeemed

of humankind, the first fruits of the sacrificial offering to God and to the Lamb. [14:5)] Neither treachery nor dissembling is found in their mouths, for they are pure and beyond reproach.

[14:6)] Then I saw another Angel flying at the summit of Heaven, holding the Everlasting Gospel. He announced the Good News to all who dwelt on the face of the earth— every nation, tribe, language, and race—[14:7)] saying with a resounding voice, "Fear the Lord! Offer Him glory! For the hour of His judgment has come! Worship the Maker of Heaven and earth, of the sea and the springs of water!"

[14:8)] And a second Angel followed him, shouting, "Fallen! Fallen is Babylon! That puffed-up, haughty city! Fallen, because she made all Nations drunk with the wine of her ferocious debauchery!"

[14:9)] Then a third Angel followed both of them, crying with a booming voice, "Whoever worships the Beast or his idol, and accepts the *charagma*—the puncture mark— on forehead or hand, [14:10)] will also drink the wine of God's fury! Indeed, His wine has already been poured— full strength—into the cup of His wrath. Those with the mark will be tormented with fire and brimstone in the presence of the holy Angels and in the presence of the Lamb. [14:11)] The fuming smoke of their torture will rise up for all eternity. Those who worship the Beast and his idol,

those who accept the *charagma* of his name, will never have peace!"

14:12) Now here is the patience of the Saints; here is the keeping of the commandments of God and the faith of Jesus. 14:13) And I heard a voice from Heaven saying to me, "Write this: 'Happy and blessed are the dead, who die in the Lord at this time.'" And I heard the Spirit say, "Yes, their accomplishments shall accompany them to their rest, to their peace from all pain and suffering."

14:14) Then I looked, and behold! A brilliant white cloud, and One like the Son of Man seated upon the cloud! Upon His head was a crown of gold, and a razor-sharp sickle was in His hand. 14:15) Then out of the temple came another Angel and called out with a loud voice to Him Who was seated upon the cloud, "O, let Your sickle fly and mow them down! For now is the time for You to reap Your harvest, before the earth dries up and withers!"

14:16) Then He Who was seated upon the cloud loosed His sickle upon the earth, and the earth was cut and mown and reaped and harvested!

14:17) Then another Angel emerged from the heavenly temple with a keen-edged sickle. 14:18) And yet another Angel came forth from the altar of sacrifice, having authority over fire, and gave an ear-splitting shout to the

Angel with the keen-edged sickle, "Drive your razor-scythe into the grape-clusters of this earthly vine and strip it out! For these bunches are bursting to be plucked!"

14:19) And the Angel flung his sickle to earth, stripping earth's vineyard clean, and he heaved the harvest into the great winepress of God's fury. 14:20) And the winepress was trodden outside the city, and blood spilled out of the winepress, as high as the horses' bridles, for a length of 1,600 stadia.[9]

---

[9]Approximately 184 miles.

CHAPTER FIFTEEN

Then I saw another great and wondrous sign in Heaven: Seven Angels holding the seven final plagues, by which God's fury was brought to an end.

15:2) I saw what looked like a sea of molten glass churning with fire. On the surface of this glass sea stood all those who had triumphed over the Beast, over his idol, and over the cipher of his name. Each one played a lyre from God, 15:3) and they chanted the song of Moses, the servant of God, and the song of the Lamb, singing, "Wondrous and magnificent are Your deeds, O Lord God, Pantokrator! Righteous and true are all Your ways, O King of the Nations![10] 15:4) Who does not fear You, O Lord,

---

[10]Textus Receptus reads "King of the Saints." The oldest manuscript in existence, Codex Sinaiticus, reads "King of the ages."

and who does not glorify Your Name? For You alone are pure and holy! All the Nations shall come and worship before You, for Your ways of righteousness and judgment are now made manifest!"

15:5) After this, I saw the Sacred Shrine of the Tabernacle of Witness in Heaven open wide. 15:6) And the seven Angels of the seven plagues emerged from the Shrine, clothed in pure white linen, with golden sashes fastened across their breasts. 15:7) And one of the Four Living Beings gave each of the seven Angels a golden vial brimming with the fury of the Living God, Who is unto ages of ages. 15:8) And the Sacred Shrine was filled with the billowing smoke of God's glory and the overwhelming presence of His power—so much so that no one was able to enter the Shrine until the seven plagues of the seven Angels had run their course.

CHAPTER SIXTEEN

And I heard a deafening cry burst forth from the Shrine, commanding the seven Angels, "Go! Empty out the vials of God's fury upon the earth!"

16:2) Then the first Angel leapt forth and emptied out his vial over the earth. And all the people who bore the mark of the Beast or who worshipped his idol were afflicted by an ulcer, foul and painful.

16:3) Then the second Angel drained his vial into the sea, and the waters became like blood drained from a cadaver, and every creature in the sea died.

16:4) Then the third Angel flooded his vial into the rivers and the springs of fresh waters, and they turned into blood. 16:5) And I heard the Angel who had stricken these waters say, "O Lord, Who Is and Was, You are righteous and holy in Your judgment of all these things,

16:6) for in return for the blood that they shed of the Saints and the Prophets, You have given them blood to drink. O, how they deserve it!"

16:7) And I heard a voice from the altar of sacrifice echo, "Yes, O Lord God, Pantokrator, Your judgments are righteous and truthful!"

16:8) Then the fourth Angel drenched the sun with his vial, and the sun was let loose to char humankind with a blistering fire. 16:9) Although people were scorched by the broiling heat, they blasphemed the Name of God, Who had authority over these plagues. They did not repent. They did not turn around. They did not acknowledge God's majesty.

16:10) Then the fifth Angel spilled his vial onto the throne of the Beast, and his kingdom was mired in darkness. The people chewed their tongues in agony 16:11) and cursed the God of Heaven because of the excruciating pain of their ulcerous sores. Still they did not repent of their ways.

16:12) Then the sixth Angel plunged his vial into the great river Euphrates. And the water in the river evaporated, making a ready passage for the kings who will come from the East, from the rising of the sun.

16:13) Then I saw three foul spirits leaping frog-like out of the mouth of the Dragon, the mouth of the Beast, and

the mouth of the lying false prophet. ^{16:14)} Indeed, these demonic spirits caused many false portents and sensational phenomena, going abroad unto the world's rulers in order to assemble them for the battle on the Great Day of God Pantokrator—the Ruler of All. ^{16:15)} ("Behold! I am coming as a thief. Happy and blessed is the one who remains watchful and preserves his garments. Thus you will not walk naked and exposed, and others see you ashamed and embarrassed.") ^{16:16)} And He gathered them together to the place that is called, in Hebrew, "Armageddon."

^{16:17)} Then the seventh Angel poured out his vial into the air. And a thunderous voice sounded out of the temple of Heaven—from the throne—saying, "It is done!"

^{16:18)} Suddenly there were shouts and peals of thunder and flashes of lightning, and a great earthquake struck, the likes of which has never been seen since humans first walked the earth, so massive and terrible was the quake. ^{16:19)} And Babylon the "Great" was split into three parts, and the cities of the Gentiles collapsed in ruin. Indeed, God did not forget Babylon the pompous; He made her drink of the cup of the furious wine of His outrage. ^{16:20)} And every island fled, and the mountains could not be found. ^{16:21)} Enormous hailstones, each weighing more

than fifty pounds, came crashing down from the sky upon all humanity. And the people cursed God because of the plague of monstrous hail, for it was terrible indeed.

CHAPTER SEVENTEEN

Then one of the seven Angels who had the seven vials approached me and spoke to me, saying, "Come, and I will show you the condemnation of the great whore, who presided over many waters. 17:2) For all the rulers of the earth committed fornication with her, and the inhabitants of the earth were drunk with the wine of her immorality."

17:3) Then he carried me away in the spirit to the desert, where I saw a woman seated on a scarlet monster. It was covered with names of sacrilege and blasphemy and possessed seven heads and ten horns. 17:4) The woman was clothed in purple and scarlet, and pasted all over with gold, extravagant jewels, and pearls. In her hand she held a golden drinking cup brimming with foul

abominations and filthy, fetid lewdness.[11] 17:5) On her forehead a name was branded: "MYSTERION"—The Secret—Babylon the "Great," the mother of whores and of the abominations of the earth.

17:6) Indeed, I saw the woman drunk on the blood of the Saints and on the blood of the Martyrs of Jesus. I was amazed, looking at her—a pretentious, swollen spectacle.

17:7) "Why are you so amazed?" the Angel said to me. "I will tell you the secret of the woman, and of the Beast, the monster that props her up, the one with seven heads and ten horns: 17:8) The monster that you saw was, and is not—and is about to creep up out of the abyss and go on to his destruction. The inhabitants of the world, those whose names have not been inscribed in the Book of Life from the very foundation of the cosmos, will be enchanted when they see the Beast—that was and is not, and will be again."

17:9) (Now here is wisdom, if you have spiritual understanding.) "The seven heads are seven mountains on which the woman sits. 17:10) And there are seven kings; five have fallen, one is, and there is another yet to come. When he finally does come, he will remain for only a short time. 17:11) The Beast that was, and is not . . . he is the

---

[11]Literally, "worldly fornication," *porneias tēs gēs*, a reading found only in a minority of surviving texts.

eighth! He comes from the previous seven and goes on to his destruction.

17:12) "The ten horns that you saw, they are ten kings who have not yet exercised royal power. But they will rule as kings for one hour, in league with the Beast. 17:13) Their purpose will be one, and they will surrender their power and control to the Beast. 17:14) They will attack the Lamb, but the Lamb will triumph over them because He is Lord of Lords and King of Kings, and those who are with Him are the chosen, the elect, and the faithful.

17:15 "The waters that you saw are the masses of peoples," he continued, "the nations and languages over which the whore presides. 17:16) The ten horns that you saw, as well as the Beast—they all despise the whore. They will strip her naked and leave her desolate. They will devour her flesh and engulf her in flames. 17:17) Truly, God has allowed their intentions to execute His purpose. They will be of one mind, and each will hand over his kingdom to the Beast, until the words of God are fulfilled. Indeed, the woman that you saw is that ostentatious city that dominates the kings of the earth."

CHAPTER EIGHTEEN

After these things I saw another Angel, with great authority, descend from Heaven. The earth glowed with the brightness of his glory.

18:2) "Fallen! Fallen is Babylon the self-exalted!" he cried out with a booming voice. "Now she is nothing but a dwelling of demons and a prison for every vile spirit, a cage for all fetid and filthy fowl. 18:3) For all the Nations have swilled the wine of her raging immorality, and the kings of the earth have committed fornication with her, and the world's businessmen have enriched themselves by the brute force of her wanton pride."

18:4) And I heard another voice from Heaven that said, "O My people, flee! Get away from her! That you not be a party to her sins nor partake of her plagues! 18:5) For her

sins stick to her like glue and pile up as high as Heaven! Indeed, God has not forgotten her injustices and her guilt. 18:6) Repay her as she repaid you! Double her return twice over for what she has done! Take the cup she poured for others and pour in twice as much! 18:7) As much as she exalted herself and indulged in riotous prodigality, even so give her torments to wail over! For she said to herself, 'Here I sit, a queen and no old hag! Misery? Hah! I'll never see it!'

18:8) "Therefore, in a single day these plagues will come upon her—death, desolation, and starvation. She will be consumed by a burning fire, for the Mighty Lord God condemns her. 18:9) When the kings of the earth—those same ones who debauched and polluted themselves with her—see the conflagration swallowing her with smoke, they will howl for her and mutilate themselves. 18:10) Terror-stricken at her torments, they will keep their distance, wailing, 'Oh no! Woe for our great city, our mighty city! Babylon! In a single hour your condemnation has come!'

18:11) "The businessmen of the world, too, will howl like the grievously bereaved on her account; no longer will anyone traffic and consume their wares: 18:12) shipments of gold and silver, expensive jewels and pearls, fine linens, silks, purple and scarlet dyes, every kind of aromatic wood, every kind of object made from ivory,

rare and exotic hardwoods, bronze, iron and marble,
18:13) cinnamon, spices, different kinds of incense, myrrh,
frankincense, wine, olive oil, refined flour, wheat, cattle,
sheep, horses, transports, and lastly, human beings—
body and soul—so much chattel.

18:14) "The juicy pleasures you craved have vanished
forever. All your luxuries and entertainments have disap-
peared, never to be found again. 18:15) The businessmen
who traded in them and grew filthy rich in Babylon will
stand aside, terrified of her blistering torments. Wailing
with grief, 18:16) they will cry out, 'Oh no! Woe for our
great city! Once upon a time she was dressed in all manner of fine linen and purple and scarlet, and bedecked
with gold, lavish jewels, and pearls. 18:17) O, that in a
single hour such wealth was destroyed forever!'

"And every sea captain, and every passenger aboard a
ship, and all the sailors, and everyone whose trade is on
the high seas will keep their distance 18:18) when they see
the smoke of her cremation, and will cry out, 'Is there
anything like her, our great city?' 18:19) Scooping up great
handfuls of dust onto their heads, they will cry aloud
with tearful lamentations, 'Oh no! Woe for our great city!
From her fantastic riches all of us with ships at sea
enriched ourselves most splendidly. Now in a single hour
she is reduced to ashes!'

18:20) "Cheer, O Heaven! Rejoice, O Saints, Apostles and Prophets! For God has executed your judgment on her!" 18:21) Then a mighty Angel lifted a boulder, like a huge millstone, and hurled it into the sea, saying, "Thus shall the vaunted city, Babylon, be brutally crushed and found no more. 18:22) Never shall music be heard in you again! No more strummers of lyres and players of flutes! No more minstrels and trumpeters! None of them shall ever be heard in you again! No more artists! No more craftsmen! No more daily grind of commerce! Let none of it be heard in you again! 18:23) Not a single lamp shall ever shine in you again! The voices of lovers, of brides and bridegrooms shall fall silent! Because your merchants were important, world-renowned, because all the nations were deceived by you, addicted to your sorcery— 18:24) and inside your walls was discovered the blood of the Prophets and of the Saints, and the blood of all those slaughtered upon the earth!"

CHAPTER NINETEEN

And after these things, I heard the thundering sound of a great multitude in Heaven saying, "Alleluia to our God! His is the salvation! His the glory! His the mighty power! 19:2) For His decisions are just and true, because He judged the pompous whore who had seduced the earth with her immorality, and He avenged the blood of His servants who died by her hand.

19:3) "Alleluia!" they cried out again. "For her plumes of smoke will billow up forever!"

19:4) Then the Twenty-four Presbyters and the Four Living Beings prostrated themselves before God, seated on His throne, and worshipped Him, saying, "Amen! Alleluia!" 19:5) And a voice came from the throne saying, "O praise our God, all you His servants—all those who fear Him, the least together with the greatest."

19:6) Then I heard a sound like a great multitude, like the surge of mighty waters and the crash of great peals of thunder, saying, "Alleluia! For the Lord God Omnipotent reigns! 19:7) Let us rejoice and be glad and give Him glory! The nuptials of the Lamb have finally arrived, and His Bride has made herself ready! 19:8) And He has granted Her to be adorned with the finest pure white linen!" Truly, this white linen is woven of the righteous deeds of the Saints.

19:9) Then an Angel said to me, "Write this: 'Happy and blessed are those who are invited to the Wedding Feast of the Lamb.' These are the true words of God."

19:10) Then I fell down before his feet to worship him. "See that you don't!" he said to me. "I am your fellow servant and the fellow servant of your brothers and sisters who bear witness to Jesus. Worship God alone!" (Truly, the witness to Jesus is the spirit of prophecy.)

19:11) Then I saw Heaven opening before me, and behold! A shining white horse! He Who rides upon it is called "Faithful" and "True," and in righteousness He judges and rides into battle. 19:12) His eyes flashed like fiery flames, and the crown of His head is a thick cluster of diadems inscribed with names. And there is a Name inscribed that no one knows except Him. 19:13) And He is robed in a garment steeped in and dripping with His own

Blood, and His Name is called "The LOGOS—The WORD of God"! ^{19:14)} And the armies in Heaven followed Him on brilliant white horses, arrayed in the finest white linen.

^{19:15)} A razor-swift, dazzling double-edged sword goes out of His mouth, by which He smites the Nations; He shepherds them with a rod of iron. He treads upon the winepress of the fierce wine of God the Pantokrator's fury. ^{19:16)} And He has upon His mantle and upon His thigh a Name inscribed, "KING OF KINGS AND LORD OF LORDS"!

^{19:17)} Then I saw an Angel standing upon the sun who shouted out with a resounding voice to all the birds flying in the highest reaches of the sky, "Come on! Gather yourselves together for the great banquet of God! ^{19:18)} Consume the flesh of kings, and the flesh of generals, the flesh of the powerful, the flesh of horses and their riders, the flesh of all humankind—free and slave, small and great."

^{19:19)} Then I saw the Beast, the kings of the earth, and their armies massed together to attack the One riding upon the brilliant white horse, to do battle with His army. ^{19:20)} But the Beast was seized and captured, and with him the false prophet who had performed sensational tricks in his presence, by which he had deceived those who had accepted the *charagma* of the Beast and had worshipped

his idol. Both were hurled alive into the blazing lake of fire that churns with brimstone. 19:21) Then He Who rides on the brilliant white horse destroyed the remnants of the Beast's forces with the sword that proceeded from His mouth.

And the multitude of birds gorged on their dead flesh.

CHAPTER TWENTY

Then I saw an Angel descending from Heaven holding the key to the abyss and an enormous chain in his hand. $^{20:2)}$ He seized the Dragon, that decrepit old snake—the Devil, Satan, the Deceiver of the whole world—and bound him with shackles for a millennium. $^{20:3)}$ Then the Angel cast him into the abyss, locking it and sealing it on top of him, that he might not deceive the Nations any more, until the millennium was complete; after that he must be loosed for yet a little while.

$^{20:4)}$ Then I beheld thrones and those who sat upon them, and judgment was granted to them. And I beheld the souls of all those whose heads had been hacked off with axes because of their witness to Jesus and the word of God. These souls are the ones who never worshipped

the Beast or his idol, nor did they accept the puncture mark—the *charagma*—on their foreheads or on their hands. These souls lived and reigned with Christ for the millennium. 20:5) (The rest of the dead will not live again until the millennium is complete.) This is the first resurrection. 20:6) Happy and blessed and holy are those who share in the first resurrection! The second death will have no power over them, but they will be priests of God and priests of Christ and will reign with Him for the millennium!

20:7) When the millennium was finished, Satan was loosed from his prison. 20:8) He uncoiled to the four corners of the earth to deceive the Nations, Gog and Magog, to rally them for war; their numbers were as the sands of the sea. 20:9) And they swarmed over the whole breadth of the planet and surrounded the encampment of the Saints and the Beloved City. Then God's fire rained down on them from the sky and consumed them. 20:10) And the Devil who deceived them was hurled into the lake of fire and brimstone, where the Beast and the false prophet already were. And they will be tormented day and night for all eternity.

20:11) Then I beheld an enormous, gleaming white throne and the One Enthroned upon it. Heaven and earth fled from His presence, and their place was found no more.

20:12) And I beheld the dead, the least with the greatest, standing before the throne; and the scrolls were unfurled. And another scroll was opened—the Book of Life, and the dead were judged by what was written in the scrolls, according to their deeds.

20:13) And the sea gave up its dead, and Death and Hades gave up their dead, and each person was judged according to what he had done.

20:14) Then Death and Hades were cast into the lake of fire (this is the second death). And anyone whose name was not found inscribed in the Book of Life was also cast into the lake of fire.

CHAPTER TWENTY-ONE

Then I beheld a new Heaven and a new earth, for the first Heaven and the first earth had passed away, and the sea was no more. ^{21:2)} And I saw the Holy City, New Jerusalem, coming down from God out of Heaven as a bride, adorned and prepared for her groom.

^{21:3)} Then I heard a voice resounding from heaven, saying, "Behold! The tabernacle of God is with humankind, and He shall make His dwelling among them. They shall be His people, and God Himself shall be with them. ^{21:4)} And God shall wipe away every tear from their eyes. Death shall be no more. And there shall be no more mourning, no more crying, no more pain; for the former things have passed away."

21:5) "Behold, I make all things new," said the One seated upon the throne. Then He said to me, "Inscribe these words, for they are faithful and true."

21:6) "It is done!" He said to me. "I! The **A**lpha and the **Ω**mega, the Beginning and the End! To whomever thirsts, I will give unconditionally from the fountain of the water of life. 21:7) Those who overcome will possess all these things, and I will be their God, and they will be My children."

21:8) But as for base cowards and hateful unbelievers, murderers and molesters, idolaters and conjurers of evil spirits and all other liars, their portion will be in the lake that burns with fire and brimstone—the second death.

21:9) Then one of the seven Angels who had held the seven vials brimming with the seven last and worst plagues approached me. "Come," he said, "I will show you the Bride, the Spouse of the Lamb."

21:10) And he took me in the spirit to a soaring, steep mountain and showed me the Holy City, Jerusalem, descending from God out of Heaven, 21:11) embodying the glory of God. Her star-like radiance was like the most precious gemstone, like crystalline jasper. 21:12) The City had a massive towering wall with twelve gates, and by the gates were twelve Angels. And names were inscribed on the gates, the names of the Twelve Tribes of

the Sons of Israel.[12] 21:13) To the East were three gates, to the North three gates, to the South three gates, and to the West three gates. 21:14) And the wall of the City had twelve foundations; on each were inscribed the twelve names of the Lamb's Twelve Apostles.

21:15) And he who spoke with me had a golden measuring reed, in order to gauge the City, Her gates and wall. 21:16) The City was laid out as a perfect square, with length and width identical. The Angel measured the City with the golden reed; it was 12,000 stadia.[13] The City's length, width, and height were all equal. 21:17) And he measured the depth of the City rampart, 144 cubits,[14] according to human measurement (rather, the Angel's).

21:18) The composition of the wall was jasper; the City was pure gold, clear as glass. 21:19) The foundations of the City's wall were embellished with every kind of precious stone. The first foundation was of blood-red jasper; the second, of deep blue sapphire; the third, of chalcedony, that translucent milky quartz; the fourth, of emerald; 21:20) the fifth, of sardonyx, with alternating layers of color; the sixth, of orange-red sardius; the seventh, of pale green peridot; the eighth, of sea-green aquamarine;

---

[12] See the list of names in 7:4–8.
[13] Nearly 1,380 miles.
[14] A little over 87 yards.

the ninth, of yellow topaz; the tenth, of green-gold chrysoprase; the eleventh, of cinnamon-violet jacinth; and the twelfth, of amethyst. 21:21) The twelve gates were twelve pearls; each was made of a single pearl. The boulevard, the grand concourse of the City, was purest gold, shimmering like deep translucent glass.

21:22) But I saw no temple in the City. For the Lord God Pantokrator—the Ruler of All—and the Lamb are Her Temple. 21:23) And the City had no need of either the sun or moon to shine, for the glory of God enlightens Her, and the Lamb is Her lamp. 21:24) And the Nations will walk in Her light, and the kings of the earth will offer their glory and honor to Her. 21:25) Her gates stand open wide; they will never be shut! For there is no more night there—only day! 21:26) And they will present Her with the glory and honor of the Nations. 21:27) But nothing profane will enter into the City, neither anyone who lies or commits loathsome, hateful acts—only those who are inscribed in the Lamb's Book of Life.

CHAPTER TWENTY-TWO

Then the Angel showed me a shimmering, crystal-clear river of living water. It wells up from the throne of God and of the Lamb and cascades down 22:2) the middle of the City's boulevard, Her grand concourse. The Tree of Life overhangs either side of the river, bringing forth twelve different fruits, yielding its fruit every month. And the leaves of the Tree are for the healing of the Nations.

22:3) No longer will there be anything that is accursed or damned, for the throne of God and of the Lamb will be in the midst of the City, and His servants will worship Him. 22:4) They will see His face, and His Name will be on their foreheads. 22:5) Neither will there be night there, and they will have no need of either lamp or sunlight, for the Lord God will illumine them, and they will reign for all eternity.

22:6) Then the Angel said to me, "These words are faithful and true! Indeed, the Lord God of the spirits of the Prophets has sent His Angelic Messenger to reveal unto His servants those future events that must soon unfold."

22:7) "Behold! I come quickly! Happy and blessed is the one who holds fast to the prophetic sayings of this book!"

22:8) And I, John, am the one who saw and heard these things for myself. When the vision was finished, I fell down in worship at the feet of the Angel who had shown me these things.

22:9) But the Angel said to me, "See that you don't! I am your fellow servant and the fellow servant of your brothers and sisters the Prophets, and of those who hold fast to the words of this book. Worship God alone!"

22:10) Then he said to me, "Do not seal up the words of the prophecy of this book! Truly, the time is fast approaching! 22:11) The unjust shall remain so, and the filthy likewise. However, the righteous shall be justified all the more, as also the holy shall be sanctified all the more."

22:12) "Behold, I come quickly! My reward is with Me, to repay you according to your deeds. 22:13) I! The **A**lpha and the **Ω**mega, the First and the Last, the Beginning and the End!"

22:14) Happy and blessed are those who do His commandments. They will have the right to partake of the

Tree of Life and to enter into the City through the gates. 22:15) But the depraved and the occultists, the molesters and the murderers, the idolaters and all who are infatuated with falsehood and lies will remain outside.

22:16) "I, Jesus, have sent My Angel to testify these things to you for the sake of the Churches. I Am the Root and Scion of David, the Bright Day Star!"

22:17) And the Spirit and the Bride say, "Come!"

And let the one who hears say, "Come!"

And let whoever thirsts, come!

And all you that yearn, come and receive freely of the water of life!

22:18) I testify to every person who hears the words of prophecy in this book: If you add anything to these words, God will inflict upon you the plagues that are described in this book. 22:19) And if you remove anything from the words of this prophecy in this book, God will take from you your portion of the Tree of Life and your place in the Holy City, which are described in this book.

22:20) He who bears witness to these things says, "Yes! I come quickly!"

Amen! Yes! Come quickly, Lord Jesus!

22:21) The grace of the Lord Jesus Christ be with all the Saints. Amen!